Chicken

KÖNEMANN

C000131991

Chicken basics

Choosing and storing your chicken are just as important as preparation and will guarantee a really tasty and healthy meal.

Getting a freshly prepared meal on the table in just 30 minutes can be quite a challenge, especially when it needs to be cooked as thoroughly as chicken. But a simple checklist can make it seem effortless.

A thigh fillet, drumstick and breast fillet.

Buying. Try to choose chicken pieces with flesh that looks light pink and moist. If you are buying frozen, make sure it is solid and tightly wrapped. Free-range or corn-fed chickens tend to be smaller but are well worth buying as they usually have more flavour.

It is a good idea to put chicken down as the last item to buy on your shopping list to minimise the time it is out of the refrigerator.

Storage. Once you get home, transfer the chicken from its plastic wrap to a plate and cover it with foil before placing in your refrigerator. This will keep the meat moist and fresh. Label and date the chicken and cook it within 2 days of purchasing.

Barbecued chickens need to be taken out of the bag and left to cool

Shred the meat from the barbecued chicken.

slightly before you shred the meat from them. Store in the refrigerator if you are not using straight away.

Freezing chicken in small portions gives you the freedom to defrost a few pieces at a time as you need them. The best way to defrost chicken is to place it on a plate or tray and leave to thaw in the refrigerator, allowing 3 hours for each 500 g (1 lb).

Frozen chicken pieces or fillets can also be thawed in the microwave on the defrost setting, but this is not recommended for whole chickens, as the thawing is uneven and parts of the bird begin to cook before other parts are fully defrosted. Never refreeze chicken, and always cook it within 12 hours of thawing. Cooked chicken can be kept in the refrigerator for up to 3 days.

Preparation. Breast fillets are usually sold as a whole breast that has been skinned and removed from the

Cut the double breast into two single fillets.

bone. These can be separated into two single fillets. The recipes in this book use single fillets (each weighing about 200 g/ 6½ oz) that have had the tenderloin removed.

The tenderloin runs along the back of the breast fillet and can be easily pulled off. Keep it to use in a stir-fry.

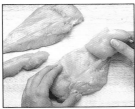

Remove the tenderloin from the back of the fillet.

Remove any excess fat or sinew from the fillet and, if you choose to leave the tenderloin on, discard the tough

Remove the membrane from the tenderloin.

white membrane at the top by holding the tip of the fillet and gently scraping it away with a sharp knife.

To cut down on cooking time, you can flatten breast and thigh fillets between 2 sheets

Flatten the fillet between 2 sheets of plastic wrap.

of plastic wrap or score them with a sharp knife. With drumsticks, make a couple of deep slashes at the top of each one. This will also assist in even cooking.

To test if chicken is cooked, insert a skewer into the thickest part of the meat. If the juices run clear, the chicken is ready. If the juices are pink, it needs a little more time. Breast fillets with the tenderloin still on may take a little longer to cook than the time given.

Making stock. Rather than discarding a barbecued or roast chicken carcass, why not use it to make chicken stock. Place the carcass in a large pan with a bouquet garni, 2 chopped onions, 2 roughly chopped carrots and 2 sticks of

celery, including the leaves. Cover with 3 litres of water, bring to the boil and simmer slowly for 3 hours, skimming off any froth with a large spoon if necessary.

Strain the stock through a fine sieve and then freeze it by putting

Strain the stock, reserving the liquid.

a plastic bag inside a measuring jug and pouring in the liquid. That way you can measure how much stock you have. When frozen, remove the bag from the jug, and seal securely before placing back in the freezer. Alternatively, pour the stock straight into ice cube trays and freeze.

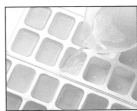

Pour the stock into ice cube trays and freeze.

3

Fast Chicken

I f you want chicken tonight without reaching for the bottled sauce, try one of these quick tasty recipes for a satisfying meal.

Chicken with Brazil Nut Butter

Ready to eat in 30 minutes
Serves 4

$^1/_2$ *cup (80 g/2$^2/_3$ oz) brazil nuts, toasted*
1 fresh red chilli, seeded and finely chopped
90 g (3 oz) butter, softened
2 tablespoons finely chopped fresh basil
4 chicken breast fillets
1 tablespoon freshly squeezed lemon juice
2 tablespoons olive oil

1. Place the brazil nuts, chilli and butter in a food processor or blender and process until combined. Transfer to a bowl and stir in the basil. Cover and refrigerate until just before serving.
2. Slash the chicken fillets deeply 3–4 times diagonally across the top. Place in a dish and coat with the lemon juice and 1 tablespoon of the oil.
3. Heat the remaining oil in a heavy-based pan. Add the chicken and cook for 3–4 minutes each side, turning once, or until cooked through. Brush a few times with the marinade during cooking. Cut each fillet into 3–4 slices.
4. Serve the chicken slices with couscous and a spoonful of the Brazil Nut Butter.

NUTRITION PER SERVE
Protein 30 g; Fat 45 g; Carbohydrate 1 g; Dietary Fibre 2 g; Cholesterol 115 mg; 2160 kJ (515 cal)

Note: Add flavour to instant couscous by stirring through 2 tablespoons finely chopped fresh parsley, 2 teaspoons grated lemon rind and 20 g ($^2/_3$ oz) butter just before serving. Season well with salt and pepper, to taste.

Chicken with Brazil Nut Butter

Peppered Chicken and Vegetables

*Ready to eat in
30 minutes
Serves 4*

5 chicken thigh fillets
  (600 g/1^1/4 lb)
^{1}/2 teaspoon green
  peppercorns
2 tablespoons oil
20 g (^{2}/3 oz) butter
2 cloves garlic, chopped
1 large carrot, chopped
2 celery sticks, sliced
3 tablespoons white
  wine
2 tablespoons cream
2 bay leaves

1. Roughly dice the
chicken. Crush the
peppercorns with the
back of a spoon and set
aside. Heat the oil and
butter in a large pan.
Cook the chicken and
garlic over high heat in
batches for about
3 minutes, or until the
chicken is browned.
2. Reduce the heat and
add the carrot and
celery. Toss well, cover
and cook for 3 minutes.
Add the wine, cream,
peppercorns and bay
leaves. Cook, covered,
for a further 5 minutes.
Season with salt and
pepper, to taste.

NUTRITION PER SERVE
*Protein 30 g; Fat 25 g;
Carbohydrate 2 g; Dietary
Fibre 1 g; Cholesterol
130 mg; 1530 kJ (365 cal)*

Note: Buy green
peppercorns in small
cans or jars from
supermarkets and
delicatessens.

Chicken and Prawn Laksa

*Ready to eat in
30 minutes
Serves 4–6*

2 tablespoons oil
2 teaspoons grated
  fresh ginger
2 cloves garlic, crushed
8 spring onions, sliced
8 chicken tenderloins,
  sliced
2–3 tablespoons mild
  curry paste
3 cups (750 ml/24 fl oz)
  hot chicken stock
1^1/2 cups (375 ml/
  12 fl oz) coconut milk
12 small raw prawns,
  peeled
150 g (5 oz) Chinese
  vermicelli
100 g (3^1/3 oz) bean
  sprouts
50 g (1^2/3 oz) snow
  peas, halved
^{1}/3 cup (20 g/^{2}/3 oz)
  chopped fresh mint
^{1}/3 cup (20 g/^{2}/3 oz)
  chopped fresh
  coriander

1. Heat the oil in a
wok. Add the ginger,
garlic and spring onion;
stir-fry for 1 minute.

Add the tenderloins to
the wok and stir-fry for
a further 2–3 minutes,
or until just cooked.
Stir in the curry paste
until the chicken is
well coated.
2. Add the hot chicken
stock and stir in the
coconut milk. Bring
slowly to the boil, then
reduce the heat and
simmer for 3 minutes.
Add the prawns and
simmer for a further
3 minutes.
3. Meanwhile, place the
vermicelli in a large
heatproof bowl and
pour over enough
boiling water to cover.
Set aside for 5 minutes,
or until soft. Drain the
vermicelli and divide
among large, warmed
serving bowls. Add the
bean sprouts and snow
peas, then ladle over
the hot laksa. Serve
sprinkled with mint
and coriander.

NUTRITION PER SERVE (6)
*Protein 40 g; Fat 35 g;
Carbohydrate 10 g; Dietary
Fibre 2 g; Cholesterol
110 mg; 2090 kJ (500 cal)*

Note: Peanut oil is
most suitable for
Asian cooking as it
withstands higher
cooking temperatures
than either olive or
vegetable oils.

*Peppered Chicken and Vegetables (top)
with Chicken and Prawn Laksa*

Poached Chicken and Ricotta Meatballs

Ready to eat in 30 minutes
Serves 4

350 g (11¹/4 oz) fine chicken mince
100 g (3¹/3 oz) fresh ricotta
¹/4 cup (35 g/1¹/4 oz) chopped black olives
2 teaspoons grated lemon rind
2 teaspoons chopped fresh oregano
1¹/2 cups (375 ml/ 12 fl oz) bottled pasta sauce
1 cup (250 ml/8 fl oz) chicken stock
1 teaspoon soft brown sugar
2 teaspoons cornflour

1. Combine the mince, ricotta, olives, rind and oregano in a bowl. Season with salt and pepper. Knead the mixture with your fingertips for about 2 minutes until well combined. With wet hands, roll quickly into small meatballs about the size of a walnut.
2. Heat the pasta sauce, stock and sugar in a large frying pan. Add the meatballs and bring to a slow boil. Simmer very gently for about 6 minutes, turning the meatballs over in the sauce a few times during cooking, until just firm.
3. Season the sauce with salt and pepper, to taste. Combine the cornflour with 1 tablespoon water. Stir in the cornflour mixture and cook until the sauce boils and thickens. Serve the sauce spooned over the meatballs.

NUTRITION PER SERVE
Protein 25 g; Fat 10 g; Carbohydrate 15 g; Dietary Fibre 3 g; Cholesterol 70 mg; 915 kJ (220 cal)

Thai-style Chicken with Coriander Mango Salsa

Ready to eat in 30 minutes
Serves 4–6

2 tablespoons oil
1 fresh red chilli, finely chopped
1 tablespoon chopped lemon grass
1 teaspoon grated fresh ginger
500 g (1 lb) chicken tenderloins, sliced
1 tablespoon light soy sauce
2 tablespoons fish sauce
¹/2 teaspoon grated palm sugar (or soft brown sugar)
¹/4 cup (60 ml/2 fl oz) lime juice
150 g (4³/4 oz) fresh Hokkien noodles

Coriander Mango Salsa
1 small onion, finely chopped
1 tablespoon chopped fresh coriander
100 g (3¹/3 oz) mango, finely diced
2 tablespoons red wine vinegar

1. Heat the oil in a pan. Add the chilli, lemon grass and ginger and cook over moderate heat for 2 minutes.
2. Add the chicken and brown for 3 minutes. Add the soy and fish sauces, sugar and lime juice. Simmer for 5 minutes, or until the chicken is cooked.
3. Meanwhile, cook the noodles in boiling water until tender. Drain, add to the pan and toss well. Serve with the Coriander Mango Salsa.
4. **To make Coriander Mango Salsa:** Combine all the ingredients in a bowl and mix well.

NUTRITION PER SERVE (6)
Protein 25 g; Fat 15 g; Carbohydrate 15 g; Dietary Fibre 1 g; Cholesterol 50 mg; 1190 kJ (285 cal)

Poached Chicken and Ricotta Meatballs (top) and Thai-style Chicken with Coriander Mango Salsa

9

Smoked Chicken Salad with Japanese Dressing

Thinly slice 3 smoked chicken breast fillets. Cut 1 small cucumber, carrot and celery stick into matchsticks. Blanch the carrot and celery for 1 minute in boiling water, then plunge into cold water and drain well. Combine the chicken, cucumber, carrot and celery. Mix in 4 sliced shiitake mushrooms, 1/2 cup (25 g/3/4 oz) chopped coriander and 3 tablespoons Japanese pickled ginger.

To make Japanese Dressing: Gently heat 2 tablespoons oil, 1/3 cup (80 ml/2 3/4 fl oz) mirin, 1 tablespoon horseradish cream, 2 teaspoons light soy sauce and 1/2 teaspoon sesame oil in a pan. Whisk to combine, then pour the dressing over the salad and sprinkle lightly with 2 tablespoons toasted sesame seeds.
Ready to eat in 30 minutes. Serves 6

NUTRITION PER SERVE
Protein 15 g; Fat 15 g; Carbohydrate 5 g; Dietary Fibre 2 g; Cholesterol 30 mg; 1000 kJ (240 cal)

Pan-fried Chicken with Vinegar

Cut 4 chicken breast fillets in half horizontally. Cover loosely with plastic wrap and pound gently with a meat mallet or rolling pin to flatten. Dust the chicken with seasoned flour (plain flour with some salt and pepper), shaking off any excess. Heat 25 g (3/4 oz) butter in a large, heavy-based pan. Add half the chicken in a single layer. Cook for 2 minutes each side, then transfer to a plate; keep warm. Repeat

with more butter and the remaining chicken. Return the chicken to the pan and add 1/3 cup (80 ml/2³/4 fl oz) balsamic vinegar. Sprinkle 2 tablespoons of chopped fresh parsley over, and serve. *Ready to eat in 20 minutes. Serves 4*

NUTRITION PER SERVE
Protein 25 g; Fat 15 g; Carbohydrate 2 g; Dietary Fibre 0 g; Cholesterol 90 mg; 960 kJ (230 cal)

From left to right: Smoked Chicken Salad with Japanese Dressing; Pan-fried Chicken with Vinegar; Pesto Chicken Pasta

Pesto Chicken Pasta

Cook 250 g (8 oz) spiral pasta in a large pan of boiling water until tender; drain. Meanwhile, remove the skin and meat from a barbecued chicken. Chop into bite-sized pieces and place in a large bowl. Add 1 cup (125 g/4 oz) toasted, roughly chopped walnuts. Grill 4 bacon

rashers until crisp; cool and roughly chop. Add the bacon, 250 g (8 oz) halved cherry tomatoes and 60 g (2 oz) pitted and sliced Kalamata olives to the chicken mixture. Add the pasta, 1/2 cup (125 g/4 oz) ready-made pesto and 1/2 cup (30 g/1 oz) shredded fresh basil. Toss together well and serve with Parmesan shavings. *Ready to eat in 30 minutes. Serves 4*

NUTRITION PER SERVE
Protein 55 g; Fat 45 g; Carbohydrate 25 g; Dietary Fibre 5 g; Cholesterol 190 mg; 3005 kJ (715 cal)

Chicken Burritos

*Ready to eat in
30 minutes
Serves 4*

Chicken Filling
*840 g (1 lb 11^1/2 oz)
can tomatoes, roughly
chopped
1 tablespoon olive oil
2 onions, diced
2 cloves garlic, crushed
^{1}/2–1 teaspoon chilli
powder
^{1}/2 teaspoon cumin
2 cups (350 g/11^1/4 oz)
shredded, cooked
chicken*

*8 flour tortillas
2 cups (130 g/4^1/4 oz)
shredded lettuce
leaves
4 tomatoes, sliced
1 small red onion,
finely sliced
1 cup (125 g/4 oz)
grated Cheddar cheese*

1. **To make Chicken
Filling:** Preheat the
oven to moderately hot
200°C (400°F/Gas 6).
Drain off half the liquid
from the canned
tomatoes. Heat the oil
in a large frying pan
and cook the onion and
garlic until soft. Add
the chilli, cumin and
tomatoes and season to
taste. Simmer for
6 minutes, or until
most of the liquid has
evaporated. Stir in the
shredded chicken and

place in a bowl. Cover
and keep warm.
2. Meanwhile, wrap the
tortillas in foil and
warm in the oven for
10 minutes. Place the
chicken mixture on the
centre of the burritos.
Arrange the lettuce,
tomato, onion and
cheese on top of the
mixture and roll up.
Alternatively, serve the
fillings in separate
bowls and let people
make up their own.

NUTRITION PER SERVE
*Protein 30 g; Fat 15 g;
Carbohydrate 40 g; Dietary
Fibre 4 g; Cholesterol
95 mg; 1840 kJ (440 cal)*

Note: Use a barbecued
chicken, leftover roast
chicken or cooked
chicken breast fillets.
Be sure to keep the
tortillas warm, as they
become dry and crusty
when cold. Once the
burritos are rolled,
wrap in paper napkins
to keep moist. Tortillas
may also be heated in
the microwave. Heat
on High (100%) for
1 minute, or until hot
and steamy.
Variation: Add some
guacamole as one of
the fillings and shake a
little Tabasco sauce
over the burrito before
rolling up.

Chicken with Mozzarella Basil Stuffing

*Ready to eat in
25 minutes
Serves 4*

*4 chicken breast fillets
2 teaspoons Dijon
mustard
4 slices mozzarella
cheese
4 large fresh basil leaves
light olive oil
125 g (4 oz) pesto*

1. Flatten the chicken
fillets between 2 sheets
of cling wrap until
2 cm (^{3}/4 inch) thick,
using a rolling pin or
meat mallet. Cut a
pocket in each fillet and
spread ^{1}/4 teaspoon
Dijon mustard around
the cavity. In each
cavity place a slice of
mozzarella and a large
basil leaf. Secure with
toothpicks.
2. Heat some light olive
oil in a frying pan.
Cook the chicken over
moderate heat for
4–6 minutes each side,
until cooked through.
Serve hot with a drizzle
of pesto sauce.

NUTRITION PER SERVE
*Protein 35 g; Fat 30 g;
Carbohydrate 5 g; Dietary
Fibre 1 g; Cholesterol
80 mg; 1730 kJ (415 cal)*

*Chicken Burritos (top)
and Chicken with Mozzarella Basil Stuffing*

Chicken Salad with Blue Cheese Croutons

Ready to eat in 30 minutes
Serves 4

1/2 French stick
75 g (2 1/2 oz) blue vein cheese (see note)
1 egg, lightly whisked
1 barbecued chicken
2 cups (360 g/11 1/2 oz) grapes, washed
1 cup (100 g/3 1/3 oz) snow pea sprouts
1/2 cup (50 g/1 2/3 oz) pecans
3/4 cup (185 g/6 oz) mayonnaise
mixed lettuce leaves, washed, to serve

1. Slice the French stick into 1 1/2 cm (5/8 inch) slices. Place on a baking tray and cook under a preheated grill until golden. Mash the cheese and egg together before spreading over one side of each slice. Grill for a further 3–5 minutes, or until golden. Cut each slice into 3–4 croutons.
2. Remove the skin and meat from the chicken. Roughly shred and combine in a bowl with the grapes, snow pea sprouts, pecans and mayonnaise. Toss the salad lightly until well combined.
3. Lay the lettuce leaves on a large platter. Spoon the chicken salad over and garnish with warm croutons.

NUTRITION PER SERVE
Protein 40 g; Fat 40 g; Carbohydrate 50 g; Dietary Fibre 5 g; Cholesterol 165 mg; 2900 kJ (690 cal)

Note: Creamy blue cheeses are more suitable as they give a more subtle flavour. For a sharper flavour, use Stilton.

Grilled Chicken Kebabs with Chilli Fruit Salsa

Ready to eat in 25 minutes
Serves 4

2 red capsicums, cubed
4 chicken breast fillets, cubed
4 bacon rashers, thickly sliced
light olive oil

Chilli Fruit Salsa
1 mango, pitted and roughly diced
1/2 cup (125 g/4 oz) plain yoghurt
juice of 2 limes
finely grated rind of 1 lime
1/3 cup (20 g/2/3 oz) chopped fresh coriander
1 jalapeño chilli, seeded and chopped

1. Preheat the grill. Thread the capsicum, chicken and bacon onto 4 long, metal skewers. Brush the kebabs with olive oil, then place under the grill. Cook, turning frequently, for about 10 minutes, or until cooked through and golden all over. Serve with the Chilli Fruit Salsa.
2. **To make the Chilli Fruit Salsa:** Combine all the salsa ingredients in a bowl. Place in the refrigerator until ready to serve.

NUTRITION PER SERVE
Protein 50 g; Fat 10 g; Carbohydrate 20 g; Dietary Fibre 3 g; Cholesterol 105 mg; 1565 kJ (375 cal)

Note: Do not pack the kebab ingredients onto the skewers too tightly or the chicken will have trouble cooking through. This recipe is also delicious cooked on the barbecue: preheat the grill plate and brush with oil before cooking. In the Chilli Fruit Salsa, a small pawpaw can be used instead of the mango, depending on what is in season.

Chicken Salad with Blue Cheese Croutons (top) and Grilled Chicken Kebabs with Chilli Fruit Salsa

Chicken with Tomato and Basil Sauce

Cut 6 chicken thigh fillets in half. Slice a red onion into rings and roughly chop 4 bacon rashers. Heat 1 tablespoon olive oil in a large, heavy-based pan, add the chicken pieces and cook over moderate-high heat for 4–5 minutes. Set aside. Reduce the heat and add 1 tablespoon olive oil. Add the onion, bacon and 2–3 crushed cloves garlic and cook for 5 minutes, until the bacon is browned. Add 425 g (13$^1/_2$ oz) can of chopped tomatoes. Stir in $^1/_2$ teaspoon each of dried basil and oregano and 1 teaspoon caster sugar. Cook over moderate heat for 4–5 minutes, until slightly reduced. Return the chicken to the pan and simmer for 10 minutes, turning once. Add 12 Kalamata olives and sprinkle with $^1/_4$ cup (15 g/$^1/_2$ oz) chopped fresh basil. *Ready to eat in 30 minutes. Serves 4*

NUTRITION PER SERVE
Protein 40 g; Fat 20 g; Carbohydrate 10 g; Dietary Fibre 5 g; Cholesterol 120 mg; 1485 kJ (355 cal)

Thai-style Chicken Cakes

Place 500 g (1 lb) chicken mince, 1 egg and 1 tablespoon cornflour in a bowl and mix well to combine. Add 2 teaspoons red curry paste, 2 finely chopped spring onions, $^1/_2$ cup (60 g/2 oz) finely sliced green beans, $^1/_4$ cup (15 g/$^1/_2$ oz) chopped fresh coriander and 1 finely chopped fresh red chilli (optional). Mix with clean hands until combined. Using wet hands, roll $^1/_4$-cup portions into balls.

Flatten to a round pattie about 8 cm (3 inches) in diameter. Add $1/2$ cm ($1/4$ inch) oil to a heavy-based pan. Cook the chicken cakes in batches for 5 minutes each side, or until cooked through. Don't let the oil get too hot as the patties burn easily. Drain on paper towels; serve with sweet chilli sauce.
Ready to eat in 30 minutes. Makes 12

NUTRITION PER SERVE
Protein 30 g; Fat 10 g; Carbohydrate 5 g; Dietary Fibre 1 g; Cholesterol 130 mg; 830 kJ (200 cal)

Chicken with Lemon, Parsley and Orecchiette

Add 375 g (12 oz) orecchiette to a large pan of boiling water and cook until tender; drain. Meanwhile, heat 1 tablespoon oil and 30 g (1 oz) butter in a large, heavy-based pan. Add 4 chicken breast fillets and cook for 3 minutes each side; set aside. Stir in $1/3$ cup (80 ml/$2^{3}/4$ fl oz) lemon juice, $1/3$ cup (20 g/$2/3$ oz) chopped fresh parsley and 30 g (1 oz) extra butter. Return the fillets to the pan; cook over low heat for 3–4 minutes, turning once, or until cooked through. During the last 2 minutes of cooking, add some lemon slices. Season with salt and pepper. Divide the pasta among heated serving plates. Top with a chicken fillet and some sauce. Garnish with fresh lemon slices and chopped fresh parsley.
Ready to eat in 30 minutes. Serves 4

NUTRITION PER SERVE
Protein 45 g; Fat 20 g; Carbohydrate 65 g; Dietary Fibre 5 g; Cholesterol 120 mg; 2750 kJ (655 cal)

From left to right: Chicken with Tomato and Basil Sauce; Thai-style Chicken Cakes; Chicken with Lemon, Parsley and Orecchiette

17

Sesame Chicken and Vegetable Stir-fry

Ready to eat in 30 minutes
Serves 4

2 tablespoons light soy
  sauce
2 tablespoons sherry
1 tablespoon grated
  fresh ginger
1–2 cloves garlic,
  crushed
1 teaspoon soft brown
  sugar
2 teaspoons sesame oil
3 chicken breast fillets,
  thinly sliced
6 spring onions
1 red capsicum
1 zucchini
1 small carrot
1 celery stick
2 tablespoons oil
1 tablespoon sesame
  seeds, toasted

1. In a large bowl, combine the soy sauce, sherry, ginger, garlic, sugar and 1 teaspoon of the sesame oil. Add the chicken; set aside. Slice the spring onions, dice the capsicum and thinly slice the zucchini, carrot and celery.
2. Drain the chicken, reserving the marinade. Pat the chicken dry with paper towels.
3. Heat 1 tablespoon of the oil and the remaining sesame oil in a wok. Add the vegetables; stir-fry for 2–3 minutes and set aside. Heat the remaining oil, add the chicken and stir-fry for 3–4 minutes, or until just cooked. Return the vegetables to the wok with the reserved marinade. Stir-fry for 2–3 minutes. Top with sesame seeds.

NUTRITION PER SERVE
Protein 30 g; Fat 15 g; Carbohydrate 10 g; Dietary Fibre 3 g; Cholesterol 60 mg; 1305 kJ (310 cal)

Chicken with Prosciutto and Bean Purée

Ready to eat in 30 minutes
Serves 4

4 chicken breast fillets
2 tablespoons olive oil
1 tablespoon freshly
  squeezed lemon juice
1 tablespoon chopped
  fresh rosemary
4 slices prosciutto

Bean Purée
400 g (12²/3 oz) can
  cannellini beans,
  drained
2 teaspoons chopped
  fresh rosemary
2 cloves garlic, crushed
2 tablespoons cream

1. Slash the chicken breasts 3–4 times diagonally across the surface. Place in a dish and coat with the combined oil, juice and rosemary. Set aside.
2. **To make Bean Purée:** Process the beans, rosemary and garlic in a food processor or blender for 15 seconds. With the motor running, add the cream. Process until smooth. Transfer to a pan and heat gently until warm.
3. Heat a little extra oil in a heavy-based pan. Add the chicken and cook for 3–4 minutes each side, turning once, until cooked through. Brush 2–3 times with the marinade during cooking. Remove the chicken, then wrap a slice of prosciutto around each fillet. Return to the pan and cook for a further 1–2 minutes, turning once. Serve with warmed Bean Purée.

NUTRITION PER SERVE
Protein 50 g; Fat 20 g; Carbohydrate 20 g; Dietary Fibre 2 g; Cholesterol 105 mg; 1985 kJ (475 cal)

Note: Cannellini beans can be replaced with canned chick peas and a little lemon juice.

Sesame Chicken and Vegetable Stir-fry (top) and Chicken with Prosciutto and Bean Purée

Herbed Chicken with Tomato Caper Sambal

Ready to eat in 30 minutes
Serves 4

16 chicken tenderloins
1 teaspoon ground sweet paprika
1 teaspoon dried thyme
1 teaspoon dried oregano
pinch of chilli powder
1/2 teaspoon freshly ground black pepper
1 tablespoon olive oil
1 tablespoon freshly squeezed lemon juice

Tomato Caper Sambal
4 large firm tomatoes, chopped
1 tablespoon baby capers
1 small red onion, finely chopped
1 clove garlic, crushed
2 teaspoons finely chopped fresh thyme
2 teaspoons finely chopped fresh oregano
1/2 teaspoon freshly ground black pepper

1. Place the chicken tenderloins in a large dish. Combine the paprika, thyme, oregano, chilli powder and pepper in a small bowl. Stir in the oil and juice to form a paste and coat the chicken with it. Set aside.

2. To make Tomato Caper Sambal: Combine all the ingredients in a bowl. Set aside.
3. Heat a little oil in a heavy-based pan and add the tenderloins. Cook for 2–3 minutes each side, turning once, until cooked through. Serve with Tomato Caper Sambal.

NUTRITION PER SERVE
Protein 75 g; Fat 15 g; Carbohydrate 5 g; Dietary Fibre 5 g; Cholesterol 160 mg; 1970 kJ (470 cal)

Mango Chicken Salad

Ready to eat in 30 minutes
Serves 4

4 chicken breast fillets
2 teaspoons olive oil
2 celery sticks, diced
2 zucchini, diced
2 green capsicums, diced
1 small fresh red chilli, seeded and chopped
1 large mango, diced
1/2 cup (80 g/2²/3 oz) unsalted macadamia nuts, lightly toasted and chopped

Dressing
1/2 cup (125 g/4 oz) whole egg mayonnaise
1 teaspoon curry powder

3/4 cup (185 g/6 oz) plain yoghurt
1 teaspoon light soy sauce
1 tablespoon chutney

1. Preheat the oven to hot 210°C (415°F/ Gas 6–7). Place the chicken breast fillets in a single layer in an ovenproof dish and lightly brush with oil. Cover with a sheet of foil and bake for 15–20 minutes, or until just cooked. Set aside to cool slightly, then cut into bite-sized pieces.
2. To make Dressing: Combine all the dressing ingredients in a small bowl and mix together well. Set aside.
3. Combine the celery, zucchini, capsicum and chilli in a large bowl. Add the chicken pieces and mix to combine. Pour over enough dressing to moisten the salad. Gently fold through the mango, taking care not to break it up. Spoon the salad onto a serving platter and sprinkle with macadamia nuts to serve.

NUTRITION PER SERVE
Protein 45 g; Fat 35 g; Carbohydrate 25 g; Dietary Fibre 5 g; Cholesterol 140 mg; 2515 kJ (600 cal)

Herbed Chicken with Tomato Caper Sambal (top) with Mango Chicken Salad

Chicken and Salad Souvlaki

Shred the skin and meat from a barbecued chicken and set aside. Rinse 100 g (3^1/3 oz) mixed salad leaves, including some rocket and set aside. Cut 4 small tomatoes into wedges. Cut 100 g (3^1/3 oz) feta cheese into cubes. Place the tomato, feta and 8 pitted Kalamata olives in a bowl. Whisk together 1 tablespoon each of olive oil and balsamic vinegar, lots of freshly ground black pepper and 1 teaspoon dried oregano in a jug. Pour over the tomato mixture and stir gently.

Combine 1–2 crushed garlic cloves and ^{1}/2 cup (125 g/4 oz) whole egg mayonnaise in a bowl and spread the mixture over 4 large pitta breads. Divide the chicken, and the salad leaves among the pitta breads. Place some tomato mixture on top. Roll up firmly, tie with string and wrap in foil to serve. *Ready to eat in 30 minutes. Makes 8*

NUTRITION PER SERVE
Protein 25 g; Fat 15 g; Carbohydrate 20 g; Dietary Fibre 2 g; Cholesterol 105 mg; 1390 kJ (330 cal)

From left to right: Chicken and Salad Souvlaki; Cream of Chicken Soup; Honey Chicken Kebabs

Cream of Chicken Soup

Remove the meat from a barbecued chicken; cover and refrigerate. Heat 60 g (2 oz) butter in a large, heavy-based pan. Add 1 chopped onion and 1 finely diced celery stick, carrot and parsnip. Cook over low heat, stirring, for 5 minutes. Add 3 tablespoons plain flour and cook, stirring, for 2 minutes. Slowly add 4 cups (1 litre) chicken stock, stirring until thickened. Slowly bring to the

boil. Boil gently for 1–2 minutes, reduce the heat and simmer for 10 minutes, or until the vegetables are cooked. Add the chicken meat, 1 cup (250 ml/8 fl oz) cream, 1/2 cup (125 ml/4 fl oz) milk and 1/3 cup (20 g/ 2/3 oz) finely chopped fresh parsley. Heat gently, without boiling. Season with salt and pepper, to taste. Serve. *Ready to eat in 30 minutes. Serves 4–6*

NUTRITION PER SERVE (6)
Protein 30 g; Fat 35 g; Carbohydrate 15 g; Dietary Fibre 2 g; Cholesterol 195 mg; 1955 kJ (465 cal)

Honey Chicken Kebabs

Cut 4 chicken breast fillets into chunks. Combine 1/4 cup (60 ml/2 fl oz) olive oil, 1–2 crushed cloves garlic, 2 teaspoons grated fresh ginger and 2 tablespoons each of honey, soy sauce and plum sauce in a bowl. Cut 2 zucchini and 1 red capsicum into chunks. Thread the chicken, zucchini and capsicum onto 8 metal skewers. Lay on a flat tray and brush with the marinade. Cook under a preheated grill or on

a barbecue flatplate for 8 minutes, or until cooked through. Turn the skewers frequently and brush often with the marinade.
Ready to eat in 30 minutes. Makes 8

NUTRITION PER SERVE
Protein 20 g; Fat 10 g; Carbohydrate 10 g; Dietary Fibre 1 g; Cholesterol 40 mg; 835 kJ (200 cal)

Hint: If you are using bamboo skewers for this recipe, soak them for 30 minutes in a bowl of cold water and drain. This will stop them burning while the kebabs are cooking.

Green Bean and Chicken Salad

*Ready to eat in
15 minutes
Serves 4*

Vinaigrette
*1/2 cup (125 ml/4 fl oz)
light olive oil
1/4 cup (60 ml/2 fl oz)
red wine vinegar
2 tablespoons
wholegrain mustard
2 spring onions, finely
chopped
salt and freshly ground
black pepper, to taste*

*750 g (1 1/2 lb) green
beans, topped and
tailed (see note)
2 cups (350 g/11 1/4 oz)
cooked chicken,
skinned, boned and
shredded
1 punnet (250 g/8 oz)
cherry tomatoes,
halved
200 g (6 1/2 oz) Gruyère
cheese, diced*

1. To make Vinaigrette:
Combine all the
vinaigrette ingredients
in a frying pan and
warm over low heat.
2. Blanch the beans in
boiling water for
4–6 minutes. Add the
chicken to the
vinaigrette. Gently
warm through.
3. Drain the beans and

add to the pan with the
tomatoes. Remove
from the heat, stir in
the Gruyère cheese and
toss lightly.

NUTRITION PER SERVE
*Protein 45 g; Fat 50 g;
Carbohydrate 5 g; Dietary
Fibre 5 g; Cholesterol
160 mg; 2765 kJ (660 cal)*

Note: 'Topped and
tailed' means to trim
both stalk ends off each
bean. Use barbecued
chicken, leftover roast
chicken or breast fillets.

Herb Crumbed Chicken Pockets

*Ready to eat in
30 minutes
Serves 4*

*4 chicken breast fillets
4 teaspoons wholegrain
mustard
4 slices Swiss cheese
4 slices smoked ham
plain flour, for dusting
2 eggs, lightly beaten
1 cup (100 g/3 1/3 oz)
dried breadcrumbs
1 teaspoon grated
lemon rind
2 tablespoons chopped
fresh parsley
oil, for frying
lemon wedges, to serve*

1. Carefully slice
horizontally through
the centre of each fillet

without cutting
all the way through.
Open out the fillet and
spread one side with
1 teaspoon of mustard.
Top with 1 slice each of
cheese and ham,
making sure they do
not overlap the edge of
the fillet. Fold over the
fillet to enclose the
filling. Thread
2 toothpicks along the
cut edge. Repeat with
the remaining fillets.
2. Place the flour and
beaten eggs in two
separate shallow bowls.
Combine the
breadcrumbs, rind and
parsley on a flat plate.
Dip the fillets in the
flour, then the egg,
then the breadcrumb
mixture.
3. Heat enough oil in a
large, heavy-based pan
to come halfway up the
side of each fillet. Add
the fillets and cook for
8 minutes, turning
once, until cooked and
golden. Drain on paper
towels, remove the
toothpicks and serve
with lemon wedges.

NUTRITION PER SERVE
*Protein 55 g; Fat 20 g;
Carbohydrate 20 g; Dietary
Fibre 2 g; Cholesterol
200 mg; 1950 kJ (465 cal)*

Hint: Leave one end of
the toothpicks clearly
showing so that they
are easy to find and
remove after cooking.

*Green Bean and Chicken Salad (top) with
Herb Crumbed Chicken Pockets*

Hot and Spicy Chicken Wings

*Ready to eat in
30 minutes
Serves 4*

12 chicken wings,
  halved
2 tablespoons sesame
  oil
1–2 fresh chillies,
  seeded and chopped
2 tablespoons fennel
  seeds
2 tablespoons sesame
  seeds
1 tablespoon grated
  fresh ginger
3 cloves garlic, crushed
2 tablespoons soy sauce
1/4 cup (60 ml/2 fl oz)
  dry sherry
1/4 cup (90 g/3 oz)
  honey

1. Trim as much fat as possible from the chicken wings using a pair of kitchen scissors.
2. Heat the oil in a heavy-based pan and stir-fry the chicken wings for 5 minutes. Add the chilli, fennel, sesame seeds, ginger and garlic. Stir-fry for 30 seconds before adding the remaining ingredients. Cover and reduce the heat to low. Cook for 12–15 minutes, stirring occasionally, until all the syrup is absorbed.
3. Serve with cooked noodles or rice.

NUTRITION PER SERVE
*Protein 15 g; Fat 20 g;
Carbohydrate 20 g; Dietary
Fibre 2 g; Cholesterol
40 mg; 1315 kJ (315 cal)*

Moroccan Chicken

*Ready to eat in
30 minutes
Serves 4–6*

1 1/2 teaspoons cumin
1 teaspoon cinnamon
1 1/2 teaspoons paprika
1 teaspoon ground
  coriander
1/4 teaspoon ground
  cloves
1/4 teaspoon cayenne
  pepper (optional)
1 teaspoon ground
  ginger
1/4 teaspoon ground
  saffron
1 1/2 teaspoons sea
  salt
2 cloves garlic, crushed
2 tablespoons freshly
  squeezed lemon juice
1 tablespoon olive oil
850 g (1 lb 11 3/4 oz)
  chicken thigh fillets
2 tablespoons oil
1 cup (250 ml/8 fl oz)
  chicken stock
250 g (8 oz) instant
  couscous
40 g (1 1/3 oz) butter
grated rind of 1 lemon
1/4 cup (30 g/1 oz)
  sultanas
2 tablespoons slivered
  almonds

1. Place the cumin, cinnamon, paprika, coriander, cloves, cayenne (if using), ginger, saffron, salt, garlic, juice and oil in a bowl. Mix well, until a smooth paste is formed.
2. Brush the paste over the chicken fillets and set aside in a bowl for at least 5 minutes.
3. Heat the oil in a frying pan over moderate heat and cook the chicken thighs with any juices for 15–20 minutes, or until cooked through.
4. Meanwhile, bring the stock to the boil in a pan and add the couscous. Cover and remove from the heat. Set aside for 5 minutes, until the stock is absorbed, then fluff with a fork to separate the grains. Stir through the butter. Add the rind, sultanas and almonds; mix well. Spoon the couscous onto heated serving plates. Slice the chicken and arrange on top of the couscous. Spoon over any pan juices and serve immediately.

NUTRITION PER SERVE (6)
*Protein 35 g; Fat 20 g;
Carbohydrate 25 g; Dietary
Fibre 2 g; Cholesterol
115 mg; 1790 kJ (425 cal)*

*Hot and Spicy Chicken Wings (top)
with Moroccan Chicken*

Chicken and Vegetables in Parchment

Preheat the oven to moderately hot 190°C (375°F/Gas 5). Cut 75 g (2¹/₂ oz) each of parsnip, carrot and green beans into matchsticks. Cut out four 30 cm (12 inch) squares of baking paper. Place a chicken breast fillet on the centre of each piece of paper. Scatter a quarter of the vegetables over each fillet. Top each

with a small sprig of thyme, a cube of butter and 1 teaspoon lemon juice. Season each with salt and pepper. Fold in the sides of the paper and scrunch the tops down to form a parcel. Lift onto an oven tray and bake for 20 minutes. Serve immediately.
Ready to eat in 30 minutes. Serves 4

NUTRITION PER SERVE
Protein 35 g; Fat 5 g; Carbohydrate 5 g; Dietary Fibre 2 g; Cholesterol 85 mg; 900 kJ (215 cal)

Piquant Chicken

Chop 6 chicken thigh fillets (about 500 g/ 1 lb) into bite-sized pieces; set aside. Heat 2 tablespoons olive oil in a large heavy-based frying pan. Add 2 chopped cloves garlic; cook for 30 seconds. Add the chicken and cook, stirring often, over high heat for 5 minutes, or until the chicken begins to brown. Add 3 diced tomatoes, 1 teaspoon dried basil and

From left to right: Chicken and Vegetables in Parchment; Piquant Chicken; Chicken, Potato and Spinach Curry

2 tablespoons each of small capers and balsamic vinegar. Bring the mixture to the boil; reduce the heat and simmer, uncovered, for 8 minutes. Stir in 2 teaspoons soft brown sugar and season with salt and freshly ground black pepper, to taste. *Ready to eat in 30 minutes. Serves 4*

NUTRITION PER SERVE
Protein 25 g; Fat 15 g; Carbohydrate 5 g; Dietary Fibre 2 g; Cholesterol 85 mg; 1110 kJ (265 cal)

Chicken, Potato and Spinach Curry

Thaw 250 g (8 oz) of frozen chopped spinach. Heat 2 tablespoons oil in a heavy-based pan. Add 1 chopped onion, 2 tablespoons Indian curry paste and 1 large diced potato. Stir over moderate-high heat for 5 minutes, or until the potato begins to brown. Add 1 cup (250 ml/8 fl oz) chicken stock and bring to a rapid boil. Add 4 chopped chicken thigh fillets (about 350 g/11^{1}/4 oz) and the spinach. Reduce the heat and simmer, covered, for 7 minutes. Season with a pinch of salt and 2 tablespoons fresh lime juice. Serve. *Ready to eat in 30 minutes. Serves 4*

NUTRITION PER SERVE
Protein 25 g; Fat 20 g; Carbohydrate 15 g; Dietary Fibre 5 g; Cholesterol 60 mg; 1305 kJ (310 cal)

Note: For a creamier curry, use coconut milk or cream instead of half the stock.

Gingered Chicken and Mushrooms

Ready to eat in 30 minutes
Serves 4–6

2 tablespoons cornflour
1 cup (250 ml/8 fl oz) chicken stock
2 tablespoons soy sauce
2 tablespoons freshly squeezed lemon juice
2 tablespoons sesame oil
4 chicken breast fillets, cut into thin strips
2 red capsicums, seeded and thinly sliced
2 tablespoons grated fresh ginger
$1/2$ cup (50 g/$1^2/3$ oz) bamboo shoots, sliced
$1^1/2$ cups (150 g/5 oz) mixed mushrooms (shiitake, oyster, flat, Swiss brown, etc), halved
2 tablespoons chopped fresh basil

1. Dissolve the cornflour in a quarter of the stock. Add the soy sauce, lemon juice and remaining stock. Set aside.
2. Heat the oil in a wok. Add the chicken, capsicum, ginger, bamboo shoots and mushrooms. Cook, stirring, for 4–6 minutes, until the chicken is cooked.
3. Stir in the liquid and basil and bring to the boil to thicken. Season with salt and pepper, to taste. Serve with steamed rice.

NUTRITION PER SERVE (6)
Protein 25 g; Fat 10 g; Carbohydrate 10 g; Dietary Fibre 1 g; Cholesterol 55 mg; 955 kJ (230 cal)

Chicken Pawpaw Salad with Ginger Dressing

Ready to eat in 30 minutes
Serves 4

4 chicken breast fillets
1 tablespoon oil
1 tablespoon light soy sauce
1 teaspoon honey
1 red capsicum, seeded
2 small zucchini
1 celery stick
3 spring onions, sliced
$1/3$ cup (20 g/$2/3$ oz) chopped fresh coriander leaves
750 g ($1^1/2$ lb) pawpaw
$1/2$ cup (80 g/$2^2/3$ oz) toasted unsalted macadamia nuts, roughly chopped

Ginger Dressing
1 tablespoon grated fresh ginger
3 tablespoons mirin
3 tablespoons oil, extra
1 tablespoon light soy sauce
2 teaspoons honey

1. Preheat the oven to hot 210°C (415°F/ Gas 6–7). Place the chicken in an ovenproof dish and coat with the combined oil, soy sauce and honey. Cover with foil and bake for 15 minutes, until tender. Cool, then slice the fillets into thin strips. Set aside.
2. Meanwhile, cut the capsicum, zucchini and celery into 5 cm (2 inch) long, thin strips. Place in a large bowl with the onion and coriander. Add the chicken; mix well. Chop the pawpaw into 2 cm ($3/4$ inch) cubes; gently stir into the salad.
3. To make Ginger Dressing: Place the ingredients in a jar and shake well to combine. Pour over the salad and carefully fold through. Scatter the macadamia nuts on top and serve.

NUTRITION PER SERVE
Protein 40 g; Fat 25 g; Carbohydrate 20 g; Dietary Fibre 5 g; Cholesterol 80 mg; 1890 kJ (450 cal)

Note: Mirin is a low alcohol sweet Japanese cooking wine made from rice.

Gingered Chicken and Mushrooms (top) and Chicken Pawpaw Salad with Ginger Dressing

Greek Chicken Salad

*Ready to eat in
30 minutes
Serves 4*

1 barbecued chicken,
  boned, skinned and
  shredded
1 cucumber, cut into
  matchsticks
150 g (4³/4 oz) feta
  cheese, diced
1/3 cup (50 g/1²/3 oz)
  pine nuts, toasted
4 tomatoes, cut into
  wedges
3 spring onions,
  chopped
1/2 cup (60 g/2 oz)
  pitted black olives
2–3 cups (70 g/2¹/3 oz)
  mixed lettuce leaves

Dressing
2/3 cup (175 ml/
  5¹/2 fl oz) light
  olive oil
2 cloves garlic, crushed
3 tablespoons black
  olive paste
1 egg yolk

1. Place the chicken,
cucumber, feta, pine
nuts, tomato, spring
onion and olives in a
large bowl; mix well
until combined.
2. To make Dressing:
Combine all the
dressing ingredients in
a jar; shake well. Pour
over the chicken
mixture; toss lightly.
3. Scatter the lettuce

leaves over a large
platter and spoon the
chicken mixture on top.

NUTRITION PER SERVE
*Protein 50 g; Fat 75 g;
Carbohydrate 5 g; Dietary
Fibre 5 g; Cholesterol
235 mg; 3770 kJ (900 cal)*

Sweet Soy Chicken with Bok Choy

*Ready to eat in
30 minutes
Serves 4*

4 bok choy
1 tablespoon oil
4 teaspoons sesame oil
2 chicken breast fillets,
  cut into thick strips
2 small fresh red
  chillies, seeded and
  finely chopped
2 teaspoons grated
  fresh ginger
6 spring onions, sliced
1 small red capsicum,
  thinly sliced
450 g (14¹/3 oz)
  Hokkien noodles
1/2 cup (25 g/³/4 oz)
  chopped fresh
  coriander
2 tablespoons kecap
  manis (see note)

1. Soak the bok choy in
a basin of cold water
for 2–3 minutes; drain.
Place in a pan of
boiling water. Simmer
for 2 minutes, then cool
under cold running

water; drain. Halve
lengthways; set aside.
2. Heat the oil with
1 teaspoon of the
sesame oil in a large
wok. Add the chicken
and stir-fry over high
heat for 3–4 minutes,
until cooked. Set aside.
3. Heat 2 teaspoons of
the sesame oil in the
wok. Add the chilli,
ginger, spring onion
and capsicum. Stir-fry
over high heat for
2–3 minutes, or until
softened. Set aside.
4. Heat the remaining
sesame oil in the wok,
then add the bok choy.
Stir-fry for 1 minute.
Set aside, keeping warm.
Meanwhile, place the
noodles in a large bowl,
cover with boiling
water and set aside.
5. Return the chicken
and vegetables to the
wok and heat through.
Add the coriander and
kecap manis; stir-fry for
2–3 minutes more.
6. Drain the noodles,
top with the chicken
mixture and serve with
bok choy.

NUTRITION PER SERVE
*Protein 30 g; Fat 15 g;
Carbohydrate 50 g; Dietary
Fibre 1 g; Cholesterol
40 mg; 1880 kJ (450 cal)*

Note: Kecap manis is a
sweet soy sauce.

*Greek Chicken Salad (top)
with Sweet Soy Chicken with Bok Choy*

Spicy Coriander Chicken

*Ready to eat in
30 minutes
Serves 4*

1 bunch (90 g/3 oz)
   fresh coriander,
   including the roots
2–3 cloves garlic
2–3 small fresh red
   chillies
1 tablespoon caster
   sugar
2 teaspoons grated lime
   rind
3 tablespoons lime juice
2 tablespoons kecap
   manis (see note)
1 tablespoon oil, plus
   2 teaspoons, extra
4 chicken breast fillets
250 g (8 oz) rice stick
   noodles
chopped fresh
   coriander leaves,
   extra, to garnish
1/2 cup (80 g/2²/3 oz)
   unsalted cashews,
   toasted, chopped

1. Wash the coriander
and shake to remove
excess water. Roughly
chop the garlic and
chillies in a food
processor or blender,
then add the coriander.
Process for a further
15 seconds. Add the
sugar, lime rind and
lime juice, kecap manis
and 1 tablespoon of the
oil. Process until
smooth.
2. Lightly score the
chicken fillets. Place in
a bowl and coat with
about one-quarter of
the coriander mixture;
set aside for 5 minutes.
3. Heat a heavy-based
pan with the extra oil.
Cook the chicken fillets
for 3–4 minutes each
side, turning once, until
cooked through. Brush
2–3 times with the
marinade while
cooking. Cut each fillet
into strips.
4. Meanwhile, cook the
noodles in a large pan
of boiling water for
5 minutes, until tender.
Drain, and pour over
most of the remaining
coriander mixture. Toss
to combine. Divide the
noodles among
4 serving plates and top
with the sliced chicken
breast and a spoonful
of the remaining
coriander mixture.
Garnish with chopped
coriander and cashews.
Serve with a green
salad, if desired.

NUTRITION PER SERVE
*Protein 40 g; Fat 20 g;
Carbohydrate 25 g; Dietary
Fibre 2 g; Cholesterol
80 mg; 1890 kJ (450 cal)*

Note: Kecap manis is a
sweet soy sauce.

Curried Chicken Sausages

*Ready to eat in
30 minutes
Serves 4*

10 chicken sausages
1¹/2 tablespoons oil
3 onions, sliced
2 cloves garlic, crushed
1–2 teaspoons curry
   powder
1 teaspoon paprika
1 teaspoon turmeric
1 cup (250 ml/8 fl oz)
   chicken stock
1/2 cup (125 ml/4 fl oz)
   apple juice
2 green apples, cored
   and roughly chopped
1 sweet potato, finely
   diced

1. Prick the sausages
and boil for 6 minutes.
Drain and thinly slice.
2. Heat the oil in a
large, heavy-based pan;
cook the onion and
garlic until soft. Add the
curry powder, paprika
and turmeric. Stir for
30 seconds before
adding the stock,
sausage, apple juice,
apples and sweet
potato. Season with salt
and pepper, to taste.
Simmer, uncovered, for
10 minutes over low
heat. Serve with rice.

NUTRITION PER SERVE
*Protein 40 g; Fat 45 g;
Carbohydrate 45 g; Dietary
Fibre 10 g; Cholesterol
135 mg; 3035 kJ (725 cal)*

*Spicy Coriander Chicken (top)
with Curried Chicken Sausages*

Parmesan Chicken with Garlic Butter

Cut 4 chicken breast fillets into thick strips. Dust with flour, shaking off any excess. Whisk together 2 eggs. In a separate bowl, combine 2 cups (160 g/5$^{1}/_{4}$ oz) fresh breadcrumbs with $^{1}/_{2}$ cup (50 g/1$^{2}/_{3}$ oz) grated fresh Parmesan cheese. Dip the chicken pieces, one at a time, into the egg, then roll in the breadcrumb mixture to coat. Heat a little oil in a frying pan. Cook the chicken in batches over moderate heat for 1–2 minutes each side, until cooked through. Drain on paper towels and keep warm. Melt 50 g (1$^{2}/_{3}$ oz) butter in a pan. Add 4 crushed cloves garlic and cook for 2–3 minutes. Add 2 tablespoons chopped fresh parsley; season to taste with salt and pepper. Pour over the warm chicken.
Ready to eat in 20 minutes. Serves 4

NUTRITION PER SERVE
Protein 40 g; Fat 20 g; Carbohydrate 30 g; Dietary Fibre 2 g; Cholesterol 190 mg; 1960 kJ (470 cal)

Chicken with Capsicum and Chilli Sauce

Cut 2 red capsicums into thin strips. Heat 2 tablespoons olive oil in a heavy-based pan. Add 1 teaspoon dried chilli flakes and the capsicum; cook over low heat for 10 minutes. Meanwhile, heat a little oil in a separate pan. Add 4 chicken breast fillets and cook for 2–3 minutes each side, until well browned.

Reduce the heat and add 2 tablespoons dry white wine. Simmer, covered, for 5 minutes. Stir 1/2 cup (125 ml/ 4 fl oz) cream into the braised capsicum and season with salt and pepper. Spoon the capsicum sauce over the chicken fillets, and sprinkle with fresh oregano leaves to serve.
*Ready to eat in
30 minutes. Serves 4*

NUTRITION PER SERVE
*Protein 30 g; Fat 30 g;
Carbohydrate 5 g; Dietary
Fibre 1 g; Cholesterol
100 mg; 1720 kJ (410 cal)*

Thai Chicken Sauté

Cut 4 chicken breast fillets into thick strips. Combine with 2 tablespoons green curry paste and 1 tablespoon oil in a bowl. Mix well and set aside for 10 minutes. Heat a heavy-based frying pan with a little oil. Cook the chicken in a single layer for about 2 minutes each side. Drizzle over 1/3 cup (80 ml/2 3/4 fl oz) coconut milk and 2 tablespoons lime juice. Turn the chicken pieces in the sauce before serving. Garnish with fresh coriander leaves for an authentic Thai flavour.
*Ready to eat in
30 minutes. Serves 4*

NUTRITION PER SERVE
*Protein 35 g; Fat 15 g;
Carbohydrate 5 g; Dietary
Fibre 0 g; Cholesterol
75 mg; 1280 kJ (305 cal)*

Note: Good quality commercial curry pastes are available from Asian food stores, delicatessens and supermarkets.

*From left to right: Parmesan Chicken
with Garlic Butter; Chicken with
Capsicum and Chilli Sauce;
Thai Chicken Sauté*

Chicken and Corn Soup

*Ready to eat in
30 minutes
Serves 6–8*

6 cups (1¹/2 litres)
  chicken stock
2 teaspoons chicken
  stock powder
440 g (14 oz) can corn
  kernels, drained
420 g (13¹/3 oz) can
  creamed corn
8 spring onions, finely
  chopped
1 tablespoon grated
  fresh ginger
3 tablespoons cornflour
2 egg whites
1 tablespoon soy sauce
2 cups (350 g/11¹/4 oz)
  shredded barbecued
  chicken

1. Combine the chicken stock, stock powder, kernels, creamed corn, three-quarters of the chopped spring onion and all the ginger in a large, heavy-based pan. Slowly bring to the boil, stirring; boil for 2 minutes.
2. Add the cornflour to 3 tablespoons water in a small bowl and mix to a smooth paste. Gradually add to the soup, stirring, until the soup boils and thickens. Simmer for 1–2 minutes.
3. Whisk together the egg whites and

2 tablespoons water in a small jug. Slowly add to the soup in a thin stream, stirring constantly to combine. Do not allow the mixture to boil.
4. Add the soy sauce and chicken. Stir to combine and simmer for 2–3 minutes, until the chicken is heated through. Garnish with the remaining chopped spring onion and serve.

NUTRITION PER SERVE (8)
*Protein 15 g; Fat 5 g;
Carbohydrate 25 g; Dietary
Fibre 5 g; Cholesterol
55 mg; 870 kJ (205 cal)*

Mixed Grill

*Ready to eat in
30 minutes
Serves 4*

Dipping Sauce
1 cup (250 g/8 oz)
  chilled mayonnaise
2 cloves garlic, crushed
1 teaspoon lemon juice
2 teaspoons chopped
  fresh basil

Marinade
¹/4 cup (60 g/2 oz)
  pesto
¹/3 cup (80 ml/
  2¹/4 fl oz) olive oil
juice of 1 lemon
¹/4 cup (25 g/³/4 oz)
  grated fresh Parmesan
  cheese

4 chicken breast or
  thigh fillets, halved
2 small eggplants,
  sliced into rounds
4 zucchini, halved
2 red capsicums,
  quartered
2 corn cobs, quartered
2 tomatoes, halved

1. To make Dipping Sauce: Combine all the dipping sauce ingredients in a small bowl. Chill until ready to use.
2. To make Marinade: Place the ingredients in a jar and shake well to combine.
3. Preheat the grill. Brush the chicken and vegetables with the marinade. Place the chicken, eggplant, zucchini, capsicum, and corn on the grill. Set the tomatoes aside.
4. Once the vegetables are starting to soften, add the tomatoes (they will take less time to cook). When the chicken and vegetables are cooked through and golden on all sides, remove from the heat. Serve immediately with Dipping Sauce.

NUTRITION PER SERVE
*Protein 45 g; Fat 5 g;
Carbohydrate 35 g; Dietary
Fibre 10 g; Cholesterol
80 mg; 1625 kJ (390 cal)*

*Chicken and Corn Soup (top)
with Mixed Grill*

Chicken and Cheese Pizza

*Ready to eat in
30 minutes
Serves 4*

Topping
1 cup (175 g/5²/3 oz)
  shredded barbecued
  chicken
1 cup (125 g/4 oz)
  grated Cheddar cheese
1 teaspoon paprika
¹/4 cup (70 g/2¹/3 oz)
  mango chutney
1 egg yolk
2 tablespoons chopped,
  fresh coriander

3 cups (375 g/12 oz)
  self-raising flour
1 teaspoon salt
60 g (2 oz) butter
1 cup (250 ml/8 fl oz)
  milk

1. Preheat the oven to
hot 220°C (425°F/
Gas 7).
2. **To make Topping:**
Combine the topping
ingredients together in
a bowl and set aside.
3. Process the flour, salt
and butter in a food
processor or blender
until the mixture
resembles coarse
breadcrumbs. Transfer
to a bowl. Add ³/4 cup
(185 ml/6 fl oz) milk
and mix gently with a
knife. Add the

remaining milk if
necessary.
4. Turn the dough out
onto a lightly floured
board and roll to line
the base of a large pizza
tray. Spread the chicken
mixture over the dough.
Bake for 10–12
minutes. Serve warm,
cut into wedges.

NUTRITION PER SERVE
*Protein 35 g; Fat 30 g;
Carbohydrate 80 g; Dietary
Fibre 5 g; Cholesterol
180 mg; 3055 kJ (730 cal)*

Note: For an even
quicker recipe, make
the pizza using good-
quality pizza bases
from the supermarket.

Mediterranean Chicken Salad

*Ready to eat in
30 minutes
Serves 6–8*

1 barbecued chicken,
  shredded
400 g (12²/3 oz) can
  artichoke hearts,
  drained and quartered
6 egg tomatoes,
  quartered
1 small fennel bulb,
  sliced
1 small red onion,
  sliced into thin rings
1 Lebanese cucumber,
  peeled and thickly
  sliced

12 Kalamata olives
125 g (4 oz) feta
  cheese, cubed
3 hard-boiled eggs,
  peeled and quartered
¹/3 cup (20 g/²/3 oz)
  chopped fresh basil

Garlic Dressing
¹/2 cup (125 ml/4 fl oz)
  olive oil
2 tablespoons white
  wine vinegar
1–2 cloves garlic,
  crushed
1 teaspoon Dijon
  mustard
¹/2 teaspoon dried
  oregano
¹/2 teaspoon caster
  sugar

1. Place the chicken,
artichoke, tomato,
fennel, onion,
cucumber and olives in
a large bowl and toss
to combine.
2. **To make Garlic
Dressing:** Shake all the
dressing ingredients in
a jar to combine. Pour
over the chicken
mixture and mix well.
3. Add the feta, eggs
and basil to the bowl.
Gently mix in so as not
to break up the eggs
and feta. If preferred,
arrange the eggs on
top of the salad when
ready to serve.

NUTRITION PER SERVE (8)
*Protein 25 g; Fat 25 g;
Carbohydrate 5 g; Dietary
Fibre 5 g; Cholesterol
170 mg; 1500 kJ (360 cal)*

*Chicken and Cheese Pizza (top)
with Mediterranean Chicken Salad*

Chicken Sesame Goujons with Aïoli

Cut 4 chicken breast fillets into thick strips. Place some flour on a plate with a little salt and pepper. Dust the chicken in the seasoned flour. Whisk together 2 eggs and then dip the chicken strips in the egg, one piece at a time. Combine $1^2/3$ cup (135 g/$4^1/2$ oz) fresh breadcrumbs with 2 tablespoons sesame seeds; roll the chicken in the mixture. Heat a large frying pan with 2 tablespoons oil and 30 g (1 oz) butter. Add the chicken in batches and cook for 2–3 minutes each side, until cooked through. Meanwhile, make the Aïoli by combining $1/2$ cup (125 g/4 oz) whole egg mayonnaise, 2 tablespoons finely chopped fresh parsley and 1–2 crushed cloves garlic. Serve the chicken with Aïoli and salad.
Ready to eat in 30 minutes. Serves 4

NUTRITION PER SERVE
Protein 45 g; Fat 40 g; Carbohydrate 30 g; Dietary Fibre 5 g; Cholesterol 250 mg; 2785 kJ (665 cal)

German-style Chicken with Sautéed Apple

Peel and core 2 green apples; cut into small wedges. Cut 3 chicken breast fillets (about 400 g/$12^2/3$ oz) into long thin strips. Heat 2 tablespoons oil in a heavy-based frying pan. Fry the chicken over high heat for 4 minutes, until golden; set aside. Heat 30 g (1 oz) butter in the pan. Add the apple and 2 teaspoons soft brown sugar. Cook, stirring, for 5 minutes, until the

apples are a light golden colour. Add 2 tablespoons brandy; stir until evaporated. Stir in 300 ml (9 1/2 fl oz) cream and 2 teaspoons wholegrain mustard. Return the chicken to the pan. Bring the sauce to the boil; reduce the heat and simmer for 3 minutes. Season well with salt and pepper. *Ready to eat in 30 minutes. Serves 4*

NUTRITION PER SERVE
Protein 35 g; Fat 65 g; Carbohydrate 15 g; Dietary Fibre 2 g; Cholesterol 230 mg; 3425 kJ (820 cal)

Citrus Chicken With Oregano

Preheat the oven to moderate 180°C (350°F/Gas 4). Place 500 g (1 lb) chicken tenderloins in a large baking dish. Combine 1/4 cup (60 ml/2 fl oz) olive oil, 1/3 cup (80 ml/2 3/4 fl oz) lemon juice, 2 tablespoons chopped fresh oregano in a jug, and season to taste with salt and freshly ground black

pepper. Pour the mixture over the tenderloins and turn the pieces to coat thoroughly. Bake for 15–20 minutes, or until the tenderloins are tender and cooked through. Serve with couscous or rice. *Ready to eat in 30 minutes. Serves 4*

NUTRITION PER SERVE
Protein 25 g; Fat 20 g; Carbohydrate 0 g; Dietary Fibre 0 g; Cholesterol 85 mg; 1180 kJ (280 cal)

From left to right: Chicken Sesame Goujons with Aïoli; German-style Chicken and Apple Simmer; Citrus Chicken with Oregano

43

Ginger Chicken Salad

*Ready to eat in
30 minutes
Serves 4*

4 chicken breast fillets
2 teaspoons oil
1 red capsicum
1 green capsicum
1 yellow zucchini
6 spring onions, thinly
  sliced
1/3 cup (20 g/2/3 oz)
  chopped fresh
  coriander
1/2 cup (80 g/2²/3 oz)
  toasted cashews,
  roughly chopped

Ginger Dressing
4 tablespoons oil
1 1/2 tablespoons rice
  wine vinegar
1 tablespoon honey
1 tablespoon grated
  fresh ginger
2 teaspoons light soy
  sauce

1. Preheat the oven to
hot 210°C (415°F/
Gas 6–7). Place the
chicken fillets in an
ovenproof dish in a
single layer, and lightly
brush with oil. Cover
loosely with foil and
bake for 15 minutes, or
until just cooked. Set
aside to cool slightly.
2. Meanwhile, cut the
capsicums and zucchini
into thin strips and put
in a bowl with the
spring onion and
coriander. Mix together
and set aside while
making the Ginger
Dressing.
**3. To make Ginger
Dressing:** Place all the
dressing ingredients in
a jar; shake to combine.
4. Slice the chicken
fillets into 5 cm (2 inch)
diagonal strips and add
to the vegetables.
Gently pour the
dressing over the salad,
coating the chicken and
vegetables well.
Sprinkle with cashews
to serve.

NUTRITION PER SERVE
*Protein 40 g; Fat 35 g;
Carbohydrate 15 g; Dietary
Fibre 5 g; Cholesterol
80 mg; 2260 kJ (540 cal)*

Pâté-stuffed Chicken Breast

*Ready to eat in
30 minutes
Serves 4*

4 chicken breast fillets
  (with skin left on)
4 tablespoons chicken
  liver pâté
60 g (2 oz) butter
1/2 cup (125 ml/4 fl oz)
  cream
1 teaspoon cornflour
1/4 cup (60 ml/2 fl oz)
  freshly squeezed
  lemon juice
2 tablespoons chopped
  fresh parsley

1. Lift up the skin of
the chicken (keeping it
attached to the breast)
and slip 1 tablespoon
of pâté between the
skin and the flesh of
each breast. Secure
with skewers.
2. Heat the butter in a
pan and cook both
sides of the chicken
until brown. Cover and
cook over moderate
heat for a further
12 minutes, until the
chicken is cooked.
Transfer to a hot dish.
Cover and keep warm.
3. Pour almost all the
cream into the pan with
the remaining juices
and brush down the
side of the pan.
Combine the cornflour
with the lemon juice
and remaining cream in
a cup. Stir until
smooth, add to the pan
and stir well. Add the
parsley and season to
taste with salt and
black pepper. Stir until
the sauce boils and
thickens. Spoon over
the chicken to serve.

NUTRITION PER SERVE
*Protein 40 g; Fat 35 g;
Carbohydrate 2 g; Dietary
Fibre 0 g; Cholesterol
195 mg; 2000 kJ (480 cal))*

Hint: Try using a
Grand Marnier or
black peppercorn pâté.

*Ginger Chicken Salad (top) with
Pâté-stuffed Chicken Breast*

Chicken with Couscous Tabbouleh

Ready to eat in 30 minutes
Serves 4

4 chicken breast fillets
2 tablespoons olive oil
1 tablespoon lemon juice
1 teaspoon dried oregano
300 g (10 oz) hummus

Couscous Tabbouleh
250 g (8 oz) instant couscous
1 cup (250 ml/8 fl oz) hot chicken stock
1/3 cup (80 ml/ 2 3/4 fl oz) lemon juice
2 tablespoons olive oil
4 spring onions, finely chopped
8 cherry tomatoes, quartered
1 cup (30 g/1oz) finely chopped fresh parsley
1/2 cup (25 g/3/4 oz) finely chopped fresh coriander

1. Score the chicken fillets. Place in a dish and pour over the combined oil, juice and oregano. Set aside.
2. **To make Couscous Tabbouleh:** Place the couscous in a large bowl with the hot stock. Stir, then cover and set aside. Combine the juice and oil in a jar. Season with salt and pepper; set aside.
3. Heat a heavy-based pan. Add the chicken; cook for 2 minutes each side. Reduce the heat to moderate and cook for 3–4 minutes each side, until cooked through. Brush often with the marinade.
4. Add the spring onion, tomato, parsley and coriander to the couscous. Stir through the dressing. Serve the chicken on top of the couscous with a large spoonful of hummus.

NUTRITION PER SERVE
Protein 50 g; Fat 35 g; Carbohydrate 40 g; Dietary Fibre 10 g; Cholesterol 80 mg; 2810 kJ (670 cal)

Turkish Sandwiches

Ready to eat in 30 minutes
Serves 4

2 tablespoons olive oil
2 cloves garlic, crushed
1/2 teaspoon dried oregano
pide bread, cut into 4 pieces
4 slender eggplant
12 chicken tenderloins
2 tablespoons pesto sauce
1/2 cup (125 g/4 oz) whole egg mayonnaise
4 large pieces sun-dried capsicum, drained
2 large tomatoes, sliced
Haloumi cheese, sliced

1. Preheat the grill. Combine the oil, garlic and oregano. Cut the pide bread pieces in half lengthways; brush with the oil mixture. Grill both sides until browned.
2. Cut the eggplant into quarters lengthways (leave the end attached). Brush with the oil mixture. Fan out and grill for 3–4 minutes, turning, until cooked. Set aside.
3. Brush the chicken with the oil mixture. Grill for 3–4 minutes, turning, until cooked.
4. Combine the pesto and mayonnaise.
5. Place one eggplant, a piece of sun-dried capsicum and 3 chicken tenderloins on each bread base. Top each with 2–3 tomato slices and a couple of slices of cheese. Place under the grill with the tops alongside for 1–2 minutes to warm and melt the cheese. Serve with pesto mayonnaise.

NUTRITION PER SERVE
Protein 35 g; Fat 35 g; Carbohydrate 55 g; Dietary Fibre 10 g; Cholesterol 95 mg; 2830 kJ (675 cal)

Chicken with Couscous Tabbouleh (top) with Turkish Sandwiches

Poached Chicken with Salsa Verde

*Ready to eat in
30 minutes
Serves 6*

6 chicken breast fillets
1 cup (250 ml/8 fl oz)
white wine
1 teaspoon grated
lemon rind
1 tablespoon freshly
squeezed lemon juice
a few whole peppercorns

Salsa Verde
1 cup (50 g/1²/3 oz)
fresh basil leaves
1 cup (50 g/1²/3 oz)
fresh mint leaves
2 tablespoons capers
1 tablespoon caster
sugar
1 teaspoon grated
lemon rind
1 tablespoon freshly
squeezed lemon juice
2 cloves garlic, crushed
1 slice white bread
3 anchovy fillets,
drained (optional)
1/3 cup (80 ml/
2³/4 fl oz) olive oil

1. Preheat the oven to moderate 180°C (350°F/Gas 4). Place the chicken in an ovenproof dish. Pour over the combined wine, rind, juice and peppercorns. Cook for 20 minutes, turning once, until just tender. Cover the chicken and set aside.

2. To make Salsa Verde: Place all the salsa verde ingredients, except the oil, in a food processor or blender and process until smooth. With the motor running, slowly add the oil. Serve with the chicken.

NUTRITION PER SERVE
*Protein 35 g; Fat 15 g;
Carbohydrate 5 g; Dietary
Fibre 1 g; Cholesterol
70 mg; 1380 kJ (330 cal)*

Chicken Fettucine with Mushroom Sauce

*Ready to eat in
30 minutes
Serves 4–6*

10 g (1/3 oz) Porcini
mushrooms
2 tablespoons olive oil
2 cloves garlic, crushed
200 g (6¹/2 oz) button
mushrooms, sliced
125 g (4 oz) prosciutto,
chopped
375 g (12 oz) fettucine
1/4 cup (60 ml/2 fl oz)
brandy
1 cup (250 ml/8 fl oz)
cream
1 barbecued chicken,
shredded
1 cup (155 g/5 oz)
frozen peas
1/3 cup (20 g/²/3 oz)
chopped fresh parsley

1. Place the Porcini mushrooms in a bowl and cover with boiling water. Set aside for 10 minutes, then drain, squeeze dry and chop.
2. Heat the oil in a large, heavy-based pan. Add the garlic; cook, stirring, for 1 minute over low heat. Add the button and porcini mushrooms and prosciutto and cook over low heat, stirring often, for 5 minutes.
3. Meanwhile, cook the pasta in a large pan of boiling water until tender; drain.
4. Add the brandy and cream to the mushroom mixture. Cook, stirring, over low heat for 2 minutes. Add the chicken, peas and parsley. Cook, stirring, for 4–5 minutes, until heated through. Add the chicken mixture to the hot pasta; mix well. Serve with grated fresh Parmesan, if desired.

NUTRITION PER SERVE (6)
*Protein 40 g; Fat 35 g;
Carbohydrate 45 g; Dietary
Fibre 5 g; Cholesterol
175 mg; 2775 kJ (660 cal)*

Note: If porcini mushrooms are not available, use 30 g dried Chinese mushrooms.

---

*Poached Chicken with Salsa Verde (top) and
Chicken Fettucine with Mushroom Sauce*

48

Tandoori Chicken Skewers

Cut 4 chicken breast or thigh fillets into small pieces. Combine 250 g (8 oz) plain yoghurt, 2–3 crushed cloves garlic, 2 teaspoons each of ground turmeric and cumin, 1 teaspoon ground coriander and 1/2 teaspoon cayenne pepper in a bowl. Cut 1 onion into thin wedges. Thread the chicken pieces alternately with the onion onto wooden or metal skewers. Lay the skewers on a greased, foil-lined grill tray. Brush liberally with the yoghurt marinade and cook under a preheated grill for 8 minutes, or until cooked through. Turn the skewers often and brush with marinade while cooking.
Ready to eat in 30 minutes. Serves 4

NUTRITION PER SERVE
Protein 40 g; Fat 5 g; Carbohydrate 5 g; Dietary Fibre 1 g; Cholesterol 90 mg; 970 kJ (230 cál)

Chicken in a Light Creamy Blue Sauce

Cut 4 chicken breast fillets into thick strips. Melt 50 g (12/3 oz) butter in a heavy-based pan. Add the chicken and cook for 5 minutes, stirring regularly. Move the chicken to one side and add 3/4 cup (185 ml/6 fl oz) cream, 1/2 cup (125 ml/4 fl oz) chicken stock and 100 g (31/3 oz) crumbled blue-vein cheese. Stir until the cheese has melted.

From left to right: Tandoori Chicken Skewers; Chicken in a Light Creamy Blue Sauce; Chicken Tenderloins with a Trio of Herbs

Bring to the boil; reduce the heat and simmer for 7 minutes, or until the chicken is tender, turning occasionally. Season with salt and pepper. (Test the sauce first as you may find that it is salty enough already.) Stir in 2 tablespoons chopped fresh parsley. Serve with pasta.
Ready to eat in 30 minutes. Serves 4

NUTRITION PER SERVE
Protein 30 g; Fat 40 g; Carbohydrate 2 g; Dietary Fibre 0 g; Cholesterol 175 mg; 2070 kJ (495 cal)

Chicken Tenderloins with a Trio of Herbs

Place 500 g (1 lb) chicken tenderloins and 2 tablespoons of olive oil in a bowl with plenty of salt and freshly ground black pepper. Heat a cast iron grill plate or frying pan until very hot. Cook the chicken quickly in batches for 1^{1}/2–2 minutes, turning each piece over as it browns. Transfer each batch to a bowl and keep warm. Add 3 tablespoons chopped fresh parsley, 2 teaspoons each of chopped fresh lemon thyme and oregano and 2 tablespoons lemon juice to the chicken. Toss together and serve immediately.
Ready to eat in 30 minutes. Serves 4

NUTRITION PER SERVE
Protein 25 g; Fat 15 g; Carbohydrate 0 g; Dietary Fibre 0 g; Cholesterol 85 mg; 1000 kJ (240 cal)

Sautéed Mushroom and Chicken Livers

Ready to eat in
25 minutes
Serves 4

400 g (12²/3 oz)
    chicken livers
plain flour, to dust
1 tablespoon oil
50 g (1²/3 oz) butter
1 onion, sliced
2 teaspoons fresh
    thyme (or 1 teaspoon
    dried)
1 cup (90 g/3 oz)
    mushrooms, chopped

1. Rinse the livers and remove any membrane. Toss lightly in a dish of flour. Heat the oil and butter in a heavy-based pan. Fry the livers until cooked and brown, then remove from the pan and set aside.
2. Add the onion and thyme to the pan and cook until soft. Stir in the mushrooms and cook for 2 minutes, then return the livers to the pan. Cook until heated through and season with salt and pepper, to taste.
3. Serve the mushroom and livers piled up on a dish of couscous.

NUTRITION PER SERVE
Protein 20 g; Fat 20 g;
Carbohydrate 5 g; Dietary
Fibre 1 g; Cholesterol
450 mg; 1105 kJ (265 cal)

Chicken Rolls with Mango Capsicum Salsa

Ready to eat in
30 minutes
Serves 6

6 chicken breast fillets
2 tablespoons freshly
    squeezed orange juice
2 tablespoons lime juice
1 tablespoon chopped
    fresh coriander
¹/2 teaspoon chilli
    powder
¹/4 teaspoon cayenne
    pepper
1 teaspoon caster sugar
1 tablespoon oil, plus
    2 teaspoons oil
6 large Lebanese breads
¹/2 cup (125 g/4 oz)
    light sour cream
cos lettuce leaves,
    to serve

Mango Capsicum Salsa
2 mangoes, diced
1 red capsicum, finely
    chopped
4 spring onions, finely
    chopped
1 small fresh red chilli,
    chopped (optional)
¹/2 cup (25 g/³/4 oz)
    chopped fresh
    coriander
1 teaspoon grated lime
    rind
1 tablespoon lime juice

1. Score the chicken fillets. Combine the orange and lime juices, coriander, chilli powder, cayenne, sugar and 1 tablespoon of the oil in a large dish. Place the chicken in the dish and coat thoroughly with the marinade. Set aside.
2. To make Mango Capsicum Salsa: Combine all the salsa ingredients in a large bowl. Set aside.
3. Heat a heavy-based pan with the remaining oil. Add the chicken and cook for 3–4 minutes each side, turning once, until cooked through. Brush with the marinade while cooking. Cut each fillet into strips lengthways.
4. Coat one side of the Lebanese bread with a tablespoon of sour cream. Lay a few lettuce leaves on top, then add the strips of one chicken breast and ¹/4 cup salsa. Roll the bread up firmly and repeat with the remaining breads. Serve with the remaining sour cream and Mango Capsicum Salsa.

NUTRITION PER SERVE
Protein 45 g; Fat 15 g;
Carbohydrate 75 g; Dietary
Fibre 5 g; Cholesterol
85 mg; 2600 kJ (620 cal)

Sautéed Mushroom and Chicken Livers (top) with
Chicken Rolls with Mango Capsicum Salsa

Chicken Marsala and Mushrooms

Ready to eat in
30 minutes
Serves 4–6

4 *chicken breast fillets*
50 g (1²/3 oz) *butter*
375 g (12 oz) *button*
    mushrooms,
    quartered
1 *onion, sliced*
1 *cup (250 ml/8 fl oz)*
    cream
1–2 *tablespoons*
    Marsala

1. Remove any excess fat from the chicken fillets. Heat half the butter in a large frying pan and cook the chicken fillets for 2–3 minutes each side, or until browned. Remove from the pan, cover and keep warm.
2. Add the remaining butter to the pan and cook the mushrooms and onion until soft. Stir in the cream and simmer gently for 5 minutes. Add the Marsala, season with salt and pepper, and simmer for a further 3 minutes. Return the chicken to the pan and simmer until heated through. Slice the chicken and spoon the sauce over, to serve.

Chicken Marsala and Mushrooms (top)
with Chicken with Basil and Lemon

NUTRITION PER SERVE (6)
Protein 30 g; Fat 25 g;
Carbohydrate 5 g; Dietary
Fibre 2 g; Cholesterol
125 mg; 1475 kJ (350 cal)

Chicken with Basil and Lemon

Ready to eat in
30 minutes
Serves 4

1 *cup (50 g/1²/3 oz)*
    fresh basil leaves
grated rind of 1 lemon
60 g (2 oz) *pine nuts,*
    toasted (see note)
2 *cloves garlic*
¹/4 *cup (60 ml/2 fl oz)*
    olive oil
4 *chicken breasts (with*
    skin left on)
¹/4 *cup (60 ml/2 fl oz)*
    vegetable oil
¹/2 *cup (125 ml/4 fl oz)*
    white wine
¹/2 *cup (125 ml/4 fl oz)*
    chicken stock
juice of 1 lemon
¹/4 *teaspoon sea salt*
freshly ground black
    pepper, to taste

1. Place the basil, lemon rind, pine nuts and garlic in a food processor. Process until smooth. With the motor still running, add the olive oil in a slow, steady stream until a smooth paste is formed.
2. Divide the basil mixture into four portions. Lift up the skin of each chicken breast (keeping it attached to the meat) and slip a portion of the basil mixture between the skin and flesh of each breast. Secure with a skewer or toothpick if necessary.
3. Heat the vegetable oil in a heavy-based pan and cook the chicken breasts for 2–3 minutes each side, or until well browned.
4. Pour the wine, stock and lemon juice over the chicken and season with the sea salt and pepper. Cook, covered, over very high heat for 15 minutes, turning occasionally, or until the chicken is cooked.
5. Serve on a bed of puréed potato or sweet potato with freshly steamed vegetables, if desired.

NUTRITION PER SERVE
Protein 40 g; Fat 45 g;
Carbohydrate 2 g; Dietary
Fibre 1 g; Cholesterol
80 mg; 2365 kJ (565 cal)

Note: Toast pine nuts in a non-stick frying pan over medium heat or alternatively place them on a baking tray and cook under the grill until golden brown. Keep a close eye on them, as they don't take long.

Roasted Chicken and Tomatoes with Rosemary

Preheat the oven to moderate 180°C (350°F/Gas 4). Cut 4 egg tomatoes in half lengthways; place in a baking dish. Add 1 tablespoon chopped fresh rosemary, 8 unpeeled cloves garlic, 1/4 cup (60 ml/ 2 fl oz) each of olive oil and balsamic vinegar, 2 tablespoons white wine vinegar and some freshly ground black pepper. Top 4 chicken breast fillets with a sprig of fresh rosemary. Wrap a long piece of prosciutto around, and secure the end with a toothpick. Add to the baking dish, rosemary-side up. Bake for 20 minutes. Remove the toothpicks. Serve with the tomatoes and pan juices. Squeeze the garlic flesh over the top and sprinkle with cracked black pepper. Top with shavings of fresh Parmesan cheese. *Ready to eat in 30 minutes. Serves 4*

NUTRITION PER SERVE
Protein 45 g; Fat 20 g; Carbohydrate 2 g; Dietary Fibre 2 g; Cholesterol 95 mg; 1575 kJ (375 cal)

Aparagus Chicken

Cut 4 chicken breast fillets into thirds. Cover the pieces in plastic wrap and flatten to about 1 cm (1/2 inch) thick. Heat 25 g (3/4 oz) butter and 1 tablespoon oil in a large pan. Cook the chicken in batches over moderate heat for 2–3 minutes each side, until cooked through. Remove from the pan and keep warm. Add 4 tablespoons lemon juice to the pan and simmer gently for

1 minute. Whisk in 50 g (1²/3 oz) butter in small pieces until combined. Meanwhile, steam, boil or microwave 16 fresh asparagus spears until tender but still crisp. Serve the asparagus over the chicken, drizzled with the sauce and topped with shavings of fresh Parmesan cheese. *Ready to eat in 30 minutes. Serves 4*

NUTRITION PER SERVE
Protein 40 g; Fat 25 g; Carbohydrate 2 g; Dietary Fibre 1 g; Cholesterol 135 mg; 1655 kJ (395 cal)

Chicken and Pasta Soup

Finely dice 2 chicken breast fillets, and roughly chop 1 cup (90 g/3 oz) mushrooms. Heat 2 tablespoons olive oil in a pan and cook 1 finely diced onion until soft and golden. Add the chicken, mushrooms, 180 g (5³/4 oz) dried broken-up pasta and 6 cups (1¹/2 litres) chicken stock. Bring to the boil. Reduce the heat and simmer for

10 minutes. Stir in 1 cup (35 g/1¹/4 oz) torn fresh basil leaves and season with ¹/2 teaspoon salt and freshly ground black pepper, to taste. *Ready to eat in 30 minutes. Serves 4*

NUTRITION PER SERVE
Protein 25 g; Fat 15 g; Carbohydrate 35 g; Dietary Fibre 5 g; Cholesterol 40 mg; 1480 kJ (355 cal)

Note: This is quite a chunky soup. Add more stock if preferred.

From left to right: Roasted Chicken and Tomatoes with Rosemary; Asparagus Chicken; Chicken and Pasta Soup

Chicken Stir-fry with Beans and Bamboo Shoots

*Ready to eat in
30 minutes
Serves 4*

*1 tablespoon grated
fresh ginger
5 cm (2 inch) piece
fresh lemon grass,
roughly chopped
5 cm (2 inch) piece lime
rind, roughly chopped
2–3 small fresh red
chillies, seeded
1–2 cloves garlic
2 tablespoons oil
8 chicken tenderloins
250 g (8 oz) beans, cut
into short lengths
230 g (7¹/3 oz) can
sliced bamboo shoots,
drained
140 ml (4²/3 fl oz)
coconut cream
¹/3 cup (20 g/²/3 oz)
chopped fresh
coriander*

1. Mix the ginger, lemon grass, rind, chillies and garlic in a food processor or blender for 15 seconds, then add 1 tablespoon of the oil. Process for a few seconds more. Slice the tenderloins into three lengthways. Place in a bowl and mix with the processed ingredients.
2. Heat the remaining oil in a wok. Add the chicken and stir-fry over high heat for 3–4 minutes, until the chicken is just cooked.
3. Add the beans and bamboo shoots; stir-fry for 3 minutes. Add the coconut cream and coriander; cook until heated through. Serve at once.

NUTRITION PER SERVE
*Protein 35 g; Fat 25 g;
Carbohydrate 5 g; Dietary
Fibre 5 g; Cholesterol
110 mg; 1555 kJ (370 cal)*

Chicken, Prosciutto and Sun-dried Capsicum Salad

*Ready to eat in
30 minutes
Serves 4*

*4 chicken breast fillets
2 tablespoons olive oil
2 teaspoons lemon juice
¹/2 cup (80 g/2²/3 oz)
sun-dried capsicum,
sliced
4 slices (75 g/2¹/2 oz)
prosciutto, chopped
¹/3 cup (50 g/1²/3 oz)
pine nuts, toasted
¹/3 cup (20 g/²/3 oz)
chopped fresh basil
12 pitted black olives*

Dressing
*¹/4 cup (60 ml/2 fl oz)
light olive oil
1 tablespoon balsamic
vinegar
1 teaspoon Dijon
mustard
¹/2 teaspoon caster
sugar*

1. Score the chicken breast fillets and place in a dish with 1 tablespoon of the oil and the lemon juice. Mix well.
2. Combine the capsicum, prosciutto, pine nuts, basil and olives in a bowl.
3. To make Dressing: Place the dressing ingredients in a jar and shake well to combine.
4. Heat a heavy-based pan with the extra oil. Cook the chicken for 3–4 minutes each side, or until cooked through. Brush often with the marinade during cooking. Cut each fillet into diagonal slices.
5. Place each sliced chicken fillet onto a warm serving plate. Top with a portion of the capsicum mixture, then drizzle with the Dressing. Serve warm.

NUTRITION PER SERVE
*Protein 40 g; Fat 40 g;
Carbohydrate 3 g; Dietary
Fibre 1 g; Cholesterol
90 mg; 2160 kJ (515 cal)*

*Chicken Stir-fry with Beans and Bamboo Shoots
(top) with Chicken, Prosciutto and
Sun-dried Capsicum Salad*

Chicken, Potato and Bean Salad

*Ready to eat in
25 minutes
Serves 4*

*500 g (1 lb) new
potatoes, sliced
1 clove garlic, crushed
1/3 cup (80 ml/2³/4 fl oz)
extra virgin olive oil
1 tablespoon white
wine vinegar
1 tablespoon whole egg
mayonnaise
1 teaspoon Dijon
mustard
1 bunch rocket
200 g (6¹/2 oz) baby
green beans, topped,
tailed and halved
200 g (6¹/2 oz) yellow
beans, topped, tailed
and halved
25 g (³/4 oz) butter
2–3 (500 g/1 lb)
chicken breast fillets,
chopped
2 tomatoes, finely diced
1 tablespoon tiny
capers*

1. Cook the potato in a large pan of boiling water until just tender; drain. Combine the garlic, oil, vinegar, mayonnaise and mustard in a bowl. Season with salt and pepper; set aside.
2. Meanwhile, arrange the rocket on a plate.

3. Plunge the beans into a large pan of boiling water and cook for 2 minutes. Cool in a bowl of iced water and drain. Heat the butter in a frying pan, add the chicken and cook until tender. Keep warm.
4. Combine the potato, chicken, beans and tomato and serve over the rocket. Drizzle with dressing, sprinkle with capers and serve.

NUTRITION PER SERVE
*Protein 35 g; Fat 30 g;
Carbohydrate 20 g; Dietary
Fibre 5 g; Cholesterol
80 mg; 2045 kJ (490 cal)*

Creamy Chicken with Pastry Shapes

*Ready to eat in
30 minutes
Serves 4*

*50 g (1²/3 oz) butter
2–3 chicken breast
fillets (500 g/1 lb total
weight), chopped
1 leek, finely sliced
1 tablespoon plain
flour
³/4 cup (185 ml/6 fl oz)
chicken stock
1/2 cup (125 ml/4 fl oz)
cream
³/4 cup (65 g/2¹/4 oz)
button mushrooms
1 sheet puff pastry
1 teaspoon Dijon
mustard*

1. Preheat the oven to moderately hot 200°C (400°F/Gas 6). Heat half the butter in a large pan. Add the chicken and cook until well browned. Set aside. Heat the remaining butter and add the leek. Stir until softened slightly, then cover. Allow the leek to sweat for 5 minutes.
2. Stir in the flour and cook for 1 minute. Remove from the heat and stir in the stock and cream. Return the chicken to the pan; return to the heat and continue stirring until the mixture boils and thickens. Reduce the heat. Simmer, covered, for 10 minutes. Slice the mushrooms and add to the pan. Cook for 5 minutes more.
3. Meanwhile, cut the pastry into shapes of your choice using pastry cutters. Place on a baking sheet and cook in the oven for 12 minutes, until puffed and golden.
4. Add the mustard to the chicken; season to taste with sea salt and black pepper. Place in a serving dish and top with the pastry shapes.

NUTRITION PER SERVE
*Protein 35 g; Fat 35 g;
Carbohydrate 20 g; Dietary
Fibre 2 g; Cholesterol
150 mg; 2225 kJ (530 cal)*

*Chicken, Potato and Bean Salad (top)
and Creamy Chicken with Pastry Shapes*

Chicken Livers with Artichokes

*Ready to eat in
30 minutes
Serves 4*

1 tablespoon olive oil
25 g (³/4 oz) butter
50 g (1²/3 oz) pancetta
  (or bacon), chopped
5 spring onions, finely
  sliced
500 g (1 lb) chicken
  livers, trimmed, cut
  into bite-sized pieces
2 cloves garlic, crushed
1 teaspoon flour
¹/3 cup (80 ml/2³/4 fl oz
  wine
1 tablespoon balsamic
  vinegar
2 teaspoons Dijon
  mustard
5–6 canned artichoke
  hearts, quartered
3 tablespoons finely
  chopped fresh parsley

1. Heat the olive oil
and butter in a large
frying pan. Add the
pancetta and cook over
moderate heat until
golden. Add the onion;
cook until softened.
2. Increase the heat and
add the chicken livers
and garlic. Cook for
about 4 minutes, or
until browned. Add the
flour; cook for a
further 20 seconds.
Remove from the heat
and stir in the wine,
vinegar, mustard,
artichokes and parsley.

3. Return to the heat
and stir until the
mixture boils and
thickens. Season with
salt and pepper. Serve
with noodles or rice.

NUTRITION PER SERVE
*Protein 25 g; Fat 30 g;
Carbohydrate 10 g; Dietary
Fibre 5 g; Cholesterol
600 mg; 1800 kJ (430 cal)*

Oriental Chicken Stir-fry

*Ready to eat in
30 minutes
Serves 4*

150 g (4³/4 oz) Chinese
  vermicelli
4 dried Chinese
  mushrooms
1 barbecued chicken
1 tablespoon sesame oil
150 g (4³/4 oz)
  asparagus, cut into
  short lengths
100 g (3¹/3 oz) sugar
  snap peas, trimmed
100 g (3¹/3 oz) bean
  sprouts
¹/2 cup (80 g/2²/3 oz)
  roasted, unsalted
  peanuts
¹/3 cup (20 g/²/3 oz)
  chopped fresh
  coriander

Dressing
¹/3 cup (80 ml/
  2³/4 fl oz) freshly
  squeezed lime juice
1 tablespoon oil

1 tablespoon sweet
  chilli sauce
1 tablespoon soft
  brown sugar
1 tablespoon grated
  fresh ginger
2 teaspoons fish sauce
1 teaspoon sesame oil

1. Place the vermicelli
in a bowl and pour
over boiling water to
cover. Set aside for
10 minutes. Place the
mushrooms in a bowl
and cover with boiling
water. Soak for
10 minutes, squeeze dry
and finely chop. Shred
the skin and meat from
the chicken.
2. Drain the vermicelli
and cut into shorter
lengths using scissors.
3. **To make Dressing:**
Shake the ingredients in
a jar to combine.
4. Heat the sesame oil
in a wok. Add the
mushrooms, asparagus
and peas. Stir-fry for
2 minutes. Add the
chicken, sprouts, nuts
and coriander. Stir-fry
for 2–3 minutes. Add
the Dressing and
vermicelli; stir-fry for
3–4 minutes, or until
heated through.

NUTRITION PER SERVE
*Protein 45 g; Fat 30 g;
Carbohydrate 45 g; Dietary
Fibre 5 g; Cholesterol
165 mg; 2755 kJ (660 cal)*

*Chicken Livers with Artichokes (top)
with Oriental Chicken Stir-fry*

Index